ST. JOSEPH

ST. JOSEPH

Help for Life's Emergencies

Compiled and edited
by Kathryn J. Hermes, FSP

auline
BOOKS & MEDIA
Boston

Library of Congress Cataloging-in-Publication Data

Saint Joseph : help for life's emergencies / compiled and edited by
Sister Kathryn J. Hermes.
    p. cm.
  Includes bibliographical references.
  ISBN 0-8198-7123-0 (pbk.)
  I. Joseph, Saint—Prayers and devotions. I. Hermes, Kathryn.
  BX2164.S25 2009
  242'.75—dc22

                   2009009902

Cover design by Rosana Usselmann

Cover art: St. Joseph. Galleria Palatina, Palazzo Pitti, Florence. Finsiel/
Alinari/Art Resource, NY.

Published by Pauline Books & Media, 50 Saint Paul's Avenue, Boston,
MA 02130-3491

Printed in the U.S.A.

www.pauline.org

Pauline Books & Media is the publishing house of the Daughters of St.
Paul, an international congregation of women religious serving the
Church with the communications media.

3 4 5 6 7 8 9   15 14 13 12 11

Contents

Acknowlegments

The stories in this book were gathered by Sister Barbara Gerace, FSP; Sister Margaret Charles Kerry, FSP; Sister Sharon Anne Legere, FSP; and Sister Margaret J. Obrovac, FSP.

The prayers were written or gathered by Sister Maureen George Muldowney, FSP; Sister Margaret J. Obrovac, FSP; and Sister Mary Mark Wickenhiser, FSP.

A word of special thanks to:

Sister Marianne Lorraine Trouvé, FSP, for her theological assistance;

Sister Mary Timothy Coniglio, FSP, for information about Saint Joseph's Table;

and Sister Mary Paula Kolar, FSP, for researching quotations.

Introduction

Dear Reader,

The book in your hands is about Saint Joseph, husband of Mary and foster father of Jesus Christ. If you are leafing through the pages of this book, you probably have a very special intention you are holding in your heart. Perhaps you want to sell a house. Maybe you are accompanying someone who is approaching his or her final hours on earth. You could be looking for a job or starting a business. You may have financial difficulties or be looking for protection for your family. Or perhaps you never knew your father, or your father abandoned or hurt you, and now you are looking for a second father. If so, Saint Joseph is your patron saint. As head of the Holy Family, Saint Joseph experienced many of these things in his own life, as we shall see. He is a powerful intercessor before God for our needs.

Many people today know about Saint Joseph as
a "real estate agent" — plant a statue in the front
yard of a house you are trying to sell, and you'll get
results fast. Or so the stories go. The other day a
woman told a friend of mine, also a Daughter of
Saint Paul, that twenty years ago she had urgently
needed to sell her house. She had been told by a
friend to bury a statue of Saint Joseph in her yard.
However, one of our sisters urged her instead to set
the statue in a place of honor in the home and to
say a novena to the saint asking his intercession.
Well, her house did sell, and twenty years later she
reports that she has had a strong devotion to Saint
Joseph ever since. The statue of Saint Joseph purchased so long ago is still enthroned in her home.

In our archives there is a precious book in
Italian about Saint Joseph — its binding taped and
its pages torn. A woman had purchased the book
from a Daughter of Saint Paul in 1933. Forty years
later, in 1973, she returned the book to the sisters,
stating that her devotion to Saint Joseph was strong
and that the saint had provided for her many times
when she was greatly in need. Although the book
was worn and the pages ripped, she thought someone else might still be able to use it to grow in
devotion to Saint Joseph!

This book you now hold isn't quite as old as the one she returned to us, but we hope you find it to be just as powerful a means of comfort and devotion.

Not simply a handbook on how to sell a house, this book is an essential guide to devotion to Saint Joseph. Others who have discovered the power of his intercession will lead you — through the stories of Joseph's powerful help in their moments of need — to place yourself under the guidance and protection of the head of the Holy Family. And, yes, they have sold their houses. They have found jobs. Bills have been paid when there was no money. Families have been reconciled, and loved ones have had a peaceful death. And the stories go on and on. We trust that you, too, will have your own story.

May Saint Joseph, foster father of Jesus Christ and true spouse of the Virgin Mary, lead you to a closer relationship with the Son of God whom he so lovingly provided for and protected on earth.

Sister Kathryn James Hermes, FSP

Who Is Saint Joseph?

*Saint Joseph is truly the faithful servant,
the guardian of the Lord, set by God as steward
over the whole human family.*

— Don G. Pasquali, SSP

Life of Saint Joseph

Joseph

— silent, capable, and holy;

— called by God as a young man to play the most important part in the drama of salvation after Mary, Jesus' mother;

— foster father of Jesus and protector of the Holy Family.

In the Gospels, very few details are given to us about the man God chose to raise his Son on earth. Some of the information we know about Joseph comes from legends found in writings from the first six hundred years of Christianity. The saints and great teachers of the early Church reflected on the significance, virtue, and holiness of Joseph. Great men and women have had a strong devotion to this saint up to the present time. Popes have entrusted to Saint Joseph the needs of the Church.

And then there are the stories... Stories from every century and from diverse places recount the protection of Joseph. Passed down from generation to generation and enshrined in families, religious communities, and countries, these stories reveal to us the virtues, attitudes, and qualities of Joseph.

There is, for instance, the story from the 1800s of the miraculous staircase of Our Lady of Light Chapel in Santa Fe, New Mexico. The Sisters of Loretto conducted a school in Santa Fe. Twenty years after its founding in 1853 they decided to add a chapel to the campus. It would be patterned after the Sainte Chapelle in Paris, with a vaulted ceiling, buttresses, and spires instead of the simple lines of the adobe churches of Santa Fe. Antoine Mouly and his son, architects from France who were already in Santa Fe building the Saint Francis Cathedral, were hired by the sisters to design the chapel. Five years later, when the chapel was completed, everyone realized that a dreadful mistake had been made. They had failed to build an access to the choir loft. Carpenters were consulted, but there seemed to be no solution other than installing a ladder to the choir loft or tearing down the structure, both of which were unacceptable.

Because the sisters needed the space for their growing student body, they began a novena to Saint Joseph, the patron saint of carpenters. On the last day of the novena, the story goes, a man appeared at the convent with a donkey and a toolbox. He was looking for work, he told the sisters, and he asked if he could build a staircase for the chapel. The sisters were delighted. The gray-haired man had only a hammer, a saw, and a T-square.

Months later he finished, and disappeared without waiting for pay or thanks. The superior went to the local lumberyard to at least pay for the wood, only to discover that no wood had been obtained from the yard for the staircase in the school's chapel.

The circular staircase the mysterious carpenter built is considered today to be an architectural masterpiece. It makes two complete 360-degree turns, yet has no central supporting pole as other circular staircases have. The staircase hangs with no support! Architects who have studied the staircase have said it defies the Law of Gravity. There isn't a single nail in the structure, only wooden pegs. The splicing of the wood is precise, beyond what would have been possible using the tools of that period. And even more mysteriously, the wood used in the staircase did not come from New Mexico. The sisters were convinced that the carpenter was Saint Joseph himself. The humble, quiet ways of this mysterious benefactor are exactly what one would expect of the foster father of Jesus.

So, who is Joseph?

The Bible tells us that Joseph was a "righteous man" (Mt 1:19). Several legends say Joseph was selected to be Mary's husband after his staff blossomed — a sign from God that he had chosen the young man for this responsibility. (Many statues of Saint Joseph depict him carrying a staff topped with lilies or other flowers in bloom.) In any case, the Scriptures tell us only that Mary was engaged to Joseph, and that it was in the months before the wedding was solemnized that Mary was visited by an angel. "Do not be afraid," the angel Gabriel said. "You are loved by God, and you will be the mother of God's Son" (cf. Lk 1:28–38).

This created a difficult beginning to Mary and Joseph's spousal relationship. Within a few short months of their engagement, Joseph realized that Mary was pregnant and that it was not his child. He wrestled with the heartbreak, the anger, the shattered dreams, the law. He didn't want Mary to be stoned, which was the punishment for adultery. He decided to dismiss her quietly. He did not lash out at her in anger. He wanted to treat her with compassion and goodness.

As he struggled with this difficult decision, Joseph himself was visited by an angel. In a dream he was told, "Joseph, son of David, do not be afraid to take Mary as your wife, for the child conceived in her is from the Holy Spirit. She will bear a son, and you are to name him Jesus, for he will save his people from their sins" (Mt 1:20–21). His turmoil and doubts about Mary and her child resolved, he continued the engagement despite the inevitable questions that would arise.

Next we find Joseph taking Mary with him to Bethlehem for a census. When they arrived in the ancient city of David, it was overcrowded and there was no room left for them in the places where travelers lodged. Joseph took Mary to a stable, where Jesus was born. What awe must have overtaken him in those first days and weeks of Jesus' infancy! God had chosen him to be the one to raise this child. Like any father, he would teach the boy to walk and talk and work and love and pray. But in those first days, Joseph must simply have watched, loved, and protected the tiny bundle, his heart breaking whenever the child cried! Both Joseph and Mary were learning in a new, unheard-of way the joy of serving their God.

King Herod was worried when strangers from the East came with their inquiries about the birth of "a new king." He quickly ordered the massacre of all infant boys in Bethlehem, hoping to snuff out this young rival. Again an angel woke Joseph from his sleep and told him to get up and flee, because the life of Jesus was in danger. A man of lesser faith might have responded, "You told me before that Jesus would save people from their sins, and now you're telling me that his life is in danger and he needs to be saved himself? This doesn't make sense!" Instead, Joseph got up, woke Mary, and left for Egypt just in time. Joseph was a man keenly sensitive to God's direction and completely willing to follow God's plan in his life.

For several years, exiled in a foreign country, Joseph the carpenter supported his family. He had left his business, his tools, his friends, his clients, his workshop behind in Nazareth. He began all over again. With courage he risked a new start-up in order to support his family. When Herod had died, an angel told him to return to Israel. Once again the family left their home and his business to resettle in Nazareth.

The only other thing we know about Joseph from the Scriptures is that he was still alive when Jesus was twelve. Each year the Holy Family would go up to Jerusalem for the festival of the Passover. When Jesus was twelve, he remained behind in the Temple when Mary and Joseph left for home after celebrating the Passover in Jerusalem. The custom of pilgrims traveling in separate groups of men and women made it possible for Mary and Joseph to journey an entire day before discovering the absence of their son. Frantically, they asked their friends whether they had seen Jesus. With no success, they looked for him among the groups of children playing together. When it was obvious they had left Jerusalem without him, they started back, fighting the fear that grips the heart of any parent when a child is lost.... They discovered him only after three days of retracing their steps through the city of Jerusalem. There he was, in the Temple, listening to the teachers and asking them questions, without even a trace of sorrow. In all their frustration and joy at finding him, they were met only with the words, "Why were you searching for me? Did you not know that I must be in my Father's house?" (Lk 2:49).

How those words must have struck Joseph with both pride and sorrow. His son, or rather the Father's Son who had been entrusted to him to raise and teach and love, was growing up. He would need to let go and place this precious boy into God's hands. Joseph could not shield him, he could not protect Jesus forever. Jesus was ready for his mission — to save the people from the darkness of sin and death.

Joseph was probably not alive for the Wedding of Cana, which took place at the beginning of

Jesus' public life. Only Mary is mentioned in John's Gospel. And clearly Joseph was not alive at the time of the Crucifixion, because Jesus entrusted his mother to the apostle John as guardian. The presumption is that Joseph passed away before Jesus left home. That's why he is invoked as the patron of a good death, because he would have died in the arms of both Jesus and Mary.

And that is it. That's all we know about Joseph. But in these everyday occurrences of his ordinary life are hidden tremendous lessons for those of us who love his foster Son. In the ordinary and extraordinary events and the emergencies of life, he wants to provide for us as he did for Jesus and Mary.

Devotion to Saint Joseph

When you pray to Saint Joseph you are stepping into the stream of a 2,000-year-old tradition in the Church. In its growth from the first days of Christianity until today, devotion to Saint Joseph has become a most powerful means of intercession in the Church.

In the first century, from the scant literature available, it is evident that Joseph was commemorated in connection with Jesus and Mary. It wasn't until the third century, however, that we find the first sculpture of Joseph. It is on a marble slab from a grave in the cemetery of Priscilla. It depicts the Magi adoring Jesus, who is sitting on Mary's lap. Directly behind them is Joseph, pointing to the Christmas star. Another image of Joseph is found on a triumphal arch of the Church of Saint Mary Major in Rome, built in 435 by Pope Sixtus III in memory of the Council of Ephesus, which proclaimed Mary as the Mother of God.

Joseph's memory was piously venerated in Nazareth, where a church was built in his honor by Saint Helena during the reign of the Roman emperor Constantine. In the seventh century in Egypt, a feast was instituted to honor Joseph's death. He was later included in the martyrology, a list of confessors — men and women who had professed Christ publicly in times of persecution and had persevered in their faith to the end of their lives — virgins who had forsaken marriage to love Christ alone, and martyrs who had laid down their lives because of their faith.

During the Dark Ages, the writings of the abbots of the great monasteries reveal a devotion to Mary the Mother of God and an esteem for Saint Joseph. It was in the monasteries that the beginnings of veneration for Saint Joseph as we know it today began to take shape. In this period we begin to see

Joseph called an intimate co-worker in our redemption, in the healing of the world. As early as the ninth century, local liturgical commemorations of Saint Joseph are noted for March 19, the day that would eventually become the Feast of Saint Joseph, Husband of Mary, and that we are familiar with today.

But it was only in the later Middle Ages that formal devotion to Saint Joseph began to appear. Saint Albert the Great, Saint Thomas Aquinas, Saint Bernard, Saint Bernardine of Siena, and others wrote of Saint Joseph. All later writings about Saint Joseph draw from the rich theological reflection of this period. In the sixteenth century, one of the first scholarly books devoted exclusively to the study of the life, death, and heavenly glory of Saint Joseph was written by the Dominican Isidoro Isolano, *Summary of the Gifts of Saint Joseph*. During this period, a great amount of popular spiritual writing focused on the life of Mary and veneration of her husband, Joseph.

The Council of Trent in the sixteenth century extended the feast of Joseph to the whole Catholic world. Religious orders were begun that placed themselves under Saint Joseph's patronage. Among them were the Jesuits in 1534 and the Congregation of the Sisters of Saint Joseph in 1650. A great saint famous for her devotion to Joseph was Saint Teresa of Avila, a Carmelite reformer who lived from 1515 to 1582.

In 1870, three months after the Papal States had been invaded, Pope Pius IX placed the entire Church under the protection of Saint Joseph, giving the saint the title Patron of the Universal Church. Bishops, religious superiors, cardinals, and others had requested that Saint Joseph be given this honor. From that point the Church, whose temporal fortunes had been in a pitiful state, began to grow stronger. The following year, Pius IX legislated March 19 as the Feast of Saint Joseph.

Two years later a young man in poor health knocked on the door of the Congregation of the Fathers of the Holy Cross in Canada. This man, Blessed Brother André Bessett, a Holy Cross brother from 1872 till his death in 1937, was responsible for building Saint Joseph's Oratory in the 1920s in Montreal. Today the Oratory attracts more than two million visitors a year. Brother André himself was known for the thousands of cures that were brought about through his prayers and the intercession of Saint Joseph.

In 1955, in response to the May Day celebrations for workers sponsored by the Communists, Pope Piux XII instituted the Feast of Saint Joseph the Worker. In this carpenter, who provided for the needs of Jesus and Mary by the work of his hands and the sweat of his brow, all working people have a shepherd, a defender, and a father. Joseph taught the Son of God how to work. In his carpenter shop, Jesus learned a trade — how to create, organize, plan, build, focus, and persevere at a project. From Joseph all those who work can learn virtue and obtain assistance and protection.

In 1989, John Paul II wrote the apostolic exhortation *Redemptori Custos*, urging the faithful not only to turn to Saint Joseph with greater fervor, but also to reflect on and imitate his humble, mature manner of service to others and of participating in the plan of salvation. He recalls how the hidden life of Jesus was entrusted to Saint Joseph's guardianship, and that in the love of Joseph and Mary and Jesus today's families can find both the model and the strength to live in a communion of love.

Popular Celebrations in Honor of Saint Joseph

Saint Joseph's Table

An ancient tradition called the Saint Joseph's Table goes back to the Middle Ages. A severe drought devastated Sicily, and the people were dying of famine. The peasants prayed for rain through the intercession of Saint Joseph. They promised that if God allowed it to rain they would prepare a feast in his honor to which everyone, especially the poor, would be invited. By a miracle, the rains came and the crops flourished. With the harvest the people prepared a *Tavola di San Giuseppe*, or Saint Joseph Table, to show their gratitude. Through the centuries people who have prayed to Saint Joseph for a favor use this festivity to offer their thanks, inviting the poor to their homes to take part in the feast. The "favor" requested must not be for personal gain or benefit but for the good of another.

According to the town or village of origin, the Saint Joseph Table takes many forms. It typically features rows of tables generously laden with beautifully arranged and often elaborately prepared foods, usually meatless dishes, as well as breads, cookies, pastries, and cakes. Tables may be held in places such as private homes, churches, restaurants, or social clubs. Today people open these feasts to one and all who wish to share the magnificence of their Saint Joseph Day celebration.

A statue of Saint Joseph presides over the table, which is usually blessed by a priest. The "altar" is the focal point of the table. It can be as simple as a statue and candle or as elaborate as a shrine with flowers and fabric, vegetables, wheat, and even fountains. The table then becomes also a place of pilgrimage.

One tradition calls for the children to play the roles of the Holy Family — Jesus, Mary, and Joseph. Angels and favorite saints are sometimes introduced. After the Holy Family has eaten, guests may partake of the meal. When the feast is over, the remaining food and whatever money has been donated are given to the poor.

Fava Beans

Fava beans are sometimes given to those who visit a Saint Joseph Table. The tradition of the fava bean also began in Sicily. During a famine all the crops failed except for the fava bean. It was grown originally for fodder for cattle, but it became a life-saver for the people. Even today some people carry a fava bean in their wallets in memory of the miraculous intervention of Saint Joseph. It is a reminder to pray to Saint Joseph, particularly for the needs of others.

Patron Saint

Saint Joseph is considered the patron of families, workers, unborn children, expectant parents, migrants and refugees, a peaceful death, and the universal Church. His intercession is invoked for accountants, carpenters, engineers, and craftsmen. He is invoked for persons beset by doubts or hesitations, those who have a profound interior life, and travelers.

Why We Can Trust
Saint Joseph

As Saint Joseph provided for his foster Son
and the Blessed Virgin here on earth,
so in heaven he has a corresponding charge.
He is the provider.

— Blessed James Alberione, SSP

Why Joseph?

We know we can trust someone who has training or expertise in a particular area, or whose personal experience connects with our own, or because that person simply, obviously, immensely cares about us.

So why should we trust in or pray to Saint Joseph? There is a whole liturgical calendar filled with saints — why should we go to Joseph to provide for us in our needs? Because, time and again, Saint Joseph has interceded on behalf of so many people: young and old, rich and poor, devout souls and the half-skeptical. We, too, can trust Joseph to care about us.

Go to Joseph!

Thousands of years before Saint Joseph was born, the Book of Genesis recounts the story of the youngest son of Jacob — also named Joseph — who was sold into slavery in Egypt by his jealous brothers. After he interpreted the dreams of

Pharaoh, he was released from slavery and prison and put in charge of preparations for the seven-year famine the dreams had predicted. When hunger did indeed fill the world, Egypt alone had food because of Joseph's hard work and preparation. People who came to Egypt for supplies were told by Pharaoh, "Go to Joseph!" (Gn 41:55).

The Old Testament Joseph prefigures the earthly foster father of Jesus. For every need of the Holy Family, Saint Joseph was provider and protector.

Joseph Understands Broken Hearts

Saint Joseph is the patron of those looking for a spouse, and he understands the painful experiences that can arise in the most intimate relationships. He discovered his wife was with child before they had come to live together. What betrayal he must have felt! He trusted her. He loved her. He respected her. Joseph knows what it is like to have one's heart broken by another to whom one has pledged love and respect. He understands the pain of shattered dreams, but he also shows us a path to follow in such situations. He acted with integrity, he persisted in respect, he believed God when the angel revealed to him in a dream what God was bringing about in Mary, and he surrendered his life's plans to play the part assigned him in the drama of salvation.

Joseph Is a Father

Saint Joseph taught Jesus to say "Father!" — addressing not only him but also the eternal Father. Joseph's words and his example were a mysterious link in that bond of trust and love between the child Jesus and his Father. What awe must have come over Saint Joseph as he watched his Son learn to pray the Psalms, take part in the Passover meal, or read the story of God's intervention in the history of the Chosen People. He was a hidden person who was gently, firmly, and wisely preparing Jesus for his ministry on earth. It was because Joseph had done his job well that Peter, James, John, and the other apostles saw in Jesus something that made them drop their nets, leave their homes, and give their lives over to following him and living in his presence. Joseph is an intercessor for all of our parenting needs.

Many today look for healing in their relationship with their fathers. Perhaps they have lost a father through death, divorce, or other circumstance. Maybe they carry deep wounds from emotional, sexual, or verbal abuse. Saint Joseph can be a second father to these individuals, helping them to replace what they have lost and discover the stability, safety, and security of true fatherhood.

Joseph Got Up and Went

Saint Joseph was just like us. In the midst of chaos and uncertainty, he tried to figure out what to do. "I will put Mary away quietly," he decided when he discovered she was pregnant. "I'll find a place to stay in an inn in Bethlehem," he planned when he took her with him to Bethlehem for the census. Both times God upset his plans. *"No,"* God seemed to say. *"Go and marry a pregnant virgin." "No, I've set you up for a stay in a stable tonight."* It would have been human to refuse, to argue, to debate, to throw in the towel. But Saint Joseph teaches us that if we follow God's plans — which at times may not make sense to us — wonderful things happen. Joseph can help us learn to discern God's voice amid the many other voices that try to tell us what to do: fear, pride, anxiety, ambition, jealousy. Joseph got up and went whenever the angel told him to go.

Joseph Has Connections

If we knew someone who could get us free tickets to a professional sports event so we could watch our favorite team play or to a private audience with the pope, we might take advantage of the connection to get what we wanted. Joseph is just such a powerful connection in heaven. He lived at least twelve years with Mary and Jesus — praying, conversing, sharing meals, working with them, experiencing together joys and sorrows, dreams and disappointments. Only those admitted by Joseph have access to the intimacy of the Holy Family. By turning to Joseph and asking for his intercession when we have special needs, we tear our thoughts away from the panic, negativity, or distraction into which it is so easy to fall. Living as close as he did to the two holiest persons who ever lived and the two most powerful persons in heaven, Saint Joseph has pull. Just as Jesus and Mary on earth trusted, loved, and relied on Joseph, so do they still in heaven.

Joseph Lived Through Catastrophes

Families are fragile units of society. Family emergencies arise from various kinds of catastrophes — financial difficulties or sudden illness, natural disasters or legal battles, loss of jobs, and ruined businesses. Joseph lost his business and still had to provide for Jesus and Mary in Egypt. He had left behind his home, his workshop, and most likely his best tools. He was poor and had to struggle to provide a living by hard work. His child's life was in danger from Herod, and his quick action saved Jesus' life. Saint Joseph understands the tremendous pressures we are under today as people try to raise families and make a living. Joseph teaches us dignity in our labor, trust in Providence, obedience to God's plan in our life, and a willing embrace of our vocation in life.

Joseph Had an Untimely Death

Fathers or father figures are an important and vital part of the formation of any child. Joseph probably died when Jesus was still at home and Mary a young woman. She was left to be the single parent of Jesus for the rest of his life. When Joseph was nearing death, that must have been a worry to him. He had spent his adult life caring for Jesus and Mary and providing for them. Now he had to leave them behind with no one to take his place. Joseph can be called upon by anyone dealing with the diagnosis of terminal illness and who, in an untimely manner, is forced to leave loved ones behind.

The Powerful Intercession
of Saint Joseph

Our holy patron, Saint Joseph,
has the power to assist us in all cases,
in every necessity, in every undertaking.

— SAINT THOMAS AQUINAS

Where Do We Learn
About Saint Joseph's Power?

We learn about Saint Joseph's power to provide and protect from the experience of others. Stories of Saint Joseph's intercession are told by saints, by religious communities, and by people who could be your neighbors. The stories below range from the devotion that saints have had to this great intercessor to more homespun stories of people who have prayed for his intercession and attributed to him special favors. These stories do not carry the weight of stories from Scripture, but there is a place for such "memories" in the large gathering of God's family.

Teresa of Avila, Spain

Saint Teresa of Avila is known for her lifelong devotion to Saint Joseph. Teresa was born in 1515. As a young woman — energetic, enthusiastic, and passionate — she entered the Carmelite Monastery of the Incarnation at Avila. After her profession she became ill and eventually fell into a coma for four days. Everyone around her thought she had died. After she came out of the coma, she was paralyzed for three years. During these years she learned mental prayer and bore her suffering with great patience. She attributed her cure to Saint Joseph and went on to reform the Carmelite community.

In her *Autobiography* she wrote that since the doctors were unable to cure her, she turned to Saint Joseph and found that he delivered her from this trouble and from many other troubles later in her life. Teresa remarked with astonishment that she couldn't remember ever having asked Saint Joseph for anything that he failed to obtain for her from God. It wasn't as if Saint Joseph would give her whatever she wanted, like some heavenly wonder worker. Instead, she came to see Saint Joseph as a powerful companion and provider on her journey to God. Sometimes she knew what was best for that journey, sometimes she didn't and had to trust God. But taking the long view, she came to realize that Saint Joseph provided for her exactly what she needed to come closer to Jesus and be all that he desired of her.

Though we could think of Saint Teresa as living a quiet life in a convent and entrusting her needs to Saint Joseph, this great reformer of Carmel actually had much in common with us. She founded monasteries all over Spain, bought and sold properties, led her followers in the way of spiritual growth, wrote books, dealt with lawsuits, and struggled with her peers and superiors for the acceptance of her vision. In other words, she dealt with people, money, and property issues and had struggles such as yours and mine. She wasn't afraid to ask Joseph for anything because she knew if there were something better or more important God wanted to give her, Joseph would obtain that favor for her. She knew that, like Joseph, her life was in God's hands, and that he had a dream for her and would help her carry it out.

She wrote in the *Autobiography* that just as Jesus was obedient to Saint Joseph, his foster father, while on earth, he is still obedient to Saint Joseph in heaven and does all he asks.

André Bessett, Montreal, Canada

Blessed Brother André was a Holy Cross brother known as the "miracle-worker of Mount Royal," where he was the doorkeeper of Notre Dame College (a school for boys ages seven to twelve).

His confidence in Saint Joseph inspired him to rec-
ommend this saint's devotion to anyone who came
to him with afflictions of any kind. The number of
miracles that were brought about through Brother
André and Saint Joseph's prayers spread his fame,
and eventually his supporters funded Saint Joseph's
Oratory in Montreal. A small chapel was erected in
1904, but it was soon too small to receive all the
people who came there to pray for the intercession
of Saint Joseph. In 1908 the chapel was extended,
and then again in 1910. But it was still not large
enough. In 1917, a new crypt-church was inaugu-
rated that was able to hold over a thousand people.
This, too, was not sufficient. So Brother André
devoted his efforts to building a basilica, which was
to become the largest sanctuary dedicated to Saint
Joseph.

The economic crisis of 1929 brought construction on the basilica to a halt. When he was
asked by his superiors in 1936 whether or not the
project should continue, Brother André responded:
"This is not my work; it is the work of Saint
Joseph. Put one of his statues in the middle of the
building. If he wants a roof over his head, he will
take care of it." Two months later, the Congregation had raised the funds necessary to resume

construction on the basilica and bring the project to completion.

The story is told by Moses Robert that, in 1923 or 1924, he was ill with peritonitis and the doctor had predicted he would die during the night. Brother André came to his bedside and shook his hand three times. "How do you feel?" the brother asked. Moses groaned. André squeezed his hand a second time. "Is anything wrong?" the brother asked him. Moses answered, "I feel terrible." Brother André shook his hand one more time. "Now it's going to be better," he stated. Moses felt a great weight fall away. The next day he took food, then climbed the hill of Mount Royal to visit Brother André and pray in the Oratory. The doctor was astounded. "I can cure with medicine," he exclaimed, "but Brother André can perform miracles!" Brother André and Saint Joseph.[1]

Brother André told everyone who came to him for prayers — and they came by the thousands — "Pray to Saint Joseph and I will pray with you." He considered Joseph to be a personal friend living

---

1. Story recounted in *Brother André According to Witnesses* by Bernard LaFreniere, CSC (Montreal: St. Joseph Oratory, 1990), 147– 149.

with God. In fact, in his life Joseph had always lived in the company of Christ. This daily relationship with God is what Brother André most wanted people to learn.

TIMOTHY GIACCARDO, SSP, ITALY

Blessed Timothy Giaccardo was the first priest ordained in the Society of Saint Paul, a group of priests and brothers who dedicate their lives to evangelizing through communication, founded by Blessed James Alberione in 1914. In the early years of the congregation, at the outbreak of World War I, there were many debts and few funds to meet them. Times were tough and resources next to impossible to come by. Timothy Giaccardo, who was the bursar, kept a lead statue of Saint Joseph, only about three inches tall, on his desk on top of the bills that needed to be paid. He prayed to Saint Joseph: "If you don't take care of them, it will go bad for us." Saint Joseph took care of paying the bills so well that when Timothy left that position, he passed on the statue to the next bursar.[2]

---

2. Story recounted in *James Alberione: Apostle for Our Times*, by Luigi Rolfo, SSP (New York: Alba House, 1987), 151.

Mother Paula Cordero, FSP, New York / Massachusetts

Mother Paula Cordero, a Daughter of Saint Paul (a congregation also founded by Blessed James Alberione), kept a statue of Saint Joseph in the community safe. Since she had brought the congregation to the United States during the Depression, she was accustomed to the worries — and bills — that come with caring for a large community of sisters and expanding the mission. The sisters in the United States took out a large loan in order to provide for the apostolic needs of sisters in other countries. The sisters worked hard to come up with enough money each month for the loan payments. The sisters who lived through that period with Mother Paula recall that each month, without fail, she had just the right amount of money for the payment — sometimes not a penny more.

Jane D., Pennsylvania

Jane has had a deep devotion to Saint Joseph all her married life, entrusting the health and safety of her family to the intercession of the Holy Family. In the late 1980s she and her husband purchased a home in Darby, Pennsylvania. One day she noticed the lights flickering and called the electric company.

She reported a possible electrical problem and expressed her concern for the safety of her two small children. A service man arrived, checked the electrical box outside the house, and called her out to show her what he had found. "Lady, do you realize there was a fire in this box? It should have burned your whole house down, but for some reason the fire stayed in the box." He scratched his head. "I have never seen that happen." Pointing to the sky, he added, "You must have someone up there who likes you." Jane knew it was Saint Joseph.

Twenty years and four children later, the family decided to sell the house. Her husband's company was moving quite a distance away, and it seemed like the right time to purchase a larger home. They went through three real estate agents trying to sell the house. Three years passed and nothing happened. Then they inherited a roach infestation from the property next door. They tried to speak to their neighbor but he would not even answer the door, much less work on a solution to the problem. Jane called in exterminators, but nothing seemed to help. Her children screamed every time they saw a roach, and she was worried about them catching some disease. How would she be able to sell her house with this roach problem? she wondered.

People came, looked, and left. And the house remained on the market.

One day her sister told her to make a novena to Saint Joseph. Another person told her to bury a statue of Saint Joseph in the front lawn and pray that the house would sell. She didn't like the idea of burying a statue of Saint Joseph, but in a local religious store she found a tiny statue in a plastic pouch and thought, "What would be the harm?" So she buried the statue and started the novena. On the evening of the ninth day, Jane said the prayer and told God that if he wanted the family to stay in the home, even though it had become unbearable, she would accept the suffering and would try to go on as best she could. The next day, the real estate agent called to say a woman was interested in buying the home, but at a much lower price. Jane's prayers were answered, but the house was sold at a $10,000 loss.

While she thanked Saint Joseph for selling her house, she also started praying for him to help her find a larger home that they could afford. As the family looked for houses near her husband's place of employment, they realized they couldn't afford to buy a home in that area. Then an amazing thing happened: Jane had a dream that she was standing in a large home. There were other people looking at the home, and they said to her, "This is the home where you are going to live." She had never met these people before and kept saying she couldn't afford a house like that. They kept insisting that this was the house she would purchase.

Later that day, her husband called from work and asked her to set up an appointment to look at a house he had seen for sale near the house they were living in. When Jane entered the back door, she noticed the kitchen was large, the family room was large, and the living room was large. There were two full bathrooms, four bedrooms, a linen closet (a luxury she hadn't had in her former home), two closets in the master bedroom, which had another door that opened to reveal stairs to the third floor attic. Jane couldn't believe what she was seeing. She asked the real estate agent for the name of the closest Catholic parish. "Saint Joseph's is a couple of blocks away," she responded. Jane was dumbfounded. The owner couldn't sell the house at the price listed and had dropped the price $10,000, just low enough for them to buy it.

Two months later, in the hours before dawn, the family's former home was destroyed by fire, along with that of the unapproachable neighbor. It was later discovered that he had purposely set fire to his house. If Jane's family had still been in their old home, they might not have survived, since at that hour they would all have been asleep. She attributes this miracle to Saint Joseph.

Sister Margaret K., Massachusetts

As a girl, Peggy's mom told her about her own devotion to Saint Joseph. She then gave her daughter a novena to Saint Joseph passed down in the family. When she learned that her mother had used this prayer to Saint Joseph to help find a husband — Peggy's dad, who is also named Joseph — Peggy decided that she, too, would pray for a "good husband" each day while she was in high school. She placed what she now considers their family's "miraculous" Saint Joseph statue in her bedroom window facing out. Each afternoon she knelt to pray the novena, which had "proven to be highly efficacious."

Suffice it to say that Saint Joseph knew there was only one man who could match Peggy's growing list of expectations. Praying the novena gradually led her to a deeper relationship with Jesus and eventually to her vocation as a sister in the congregation of the Daughters of Saint Paul.

When Sister Margaret entered the convent, the family statue representing Saint Joseph was claimed by her sister, who moved it into her room. One night it fell from her windowsill onto her bed. She woke in time to see a young man coming through her window. Startled, the intruder fled.

This statue, now broken in places, chipped, and missing pieces, has a place of honor in the K. home, greeting guests who enter. As Sister Margaret says, "Joseph welcomes every one of us as we are — broken, chipped, and missing pieces. Saint Joseph's great love for Mary and Jesus reflects the gift of mercy, forgiveness, and love found in Christian family life."

SUSAN AND WALTER W., ARKANSAS

Susan and Walter entrusted their family and their future to Saint Joseph. A few years ago they discovered that the roof of their house was literally about to cave in. It was leaking in all the rooms across the back of the house. They didn't have the money for a new roof, so they turned to Saint Joseph for help. They had heard how Brother André Bessett had set a statue of Saint Joseph on the floor of the unfinished basilica he was building. As there was no roof, the statue was exposed to the elements. Brother André remarked in his simple faith: "When

Saint Joseph gets tired of being rained on, he will provide the money we need to finish the dome." And sure enough, Saint Joseph did just that. Susan and Walter placed huge plastic storage bins under where the water poured in when it rained. Then they placed the statue of Saint Joseph in one of the bins and prayed: "Saint Joseph, we mean you no disrespect but, on the contrary, we wish to show you our complete trust that you will provide us with the money for a new roof after you are tired of getting wet in this rain, just as you did for Brother André and his community."

Within a few weeks, a man called them. He recounted a dream in which Jesus had said to him, "Go and help my little ones because their roof is about to cave in." Saint Joseph didn't stop with providing for the repair of the roof, but took care of many other repairs on the structure of the house as well. In time, the house became a center of prayer.

Walter placed a list of the family's more urgent needs under a new statue of Saint Joseph two years ago, and one by one, unbelievably, Joseph is checking off each item on the list: "Saint Joseph, please hear and grant our prayers for all of our financial and spiritual needs, all debt to be fully repaid, the bank loan to be repaid fully and quickly, our family and community needs — both temporal and spiritual, blessings and conversion of heart for all the members of our family and community members."

After they explained to a bishop that they had entrusted their lives and community to the care of Saint Joseph, he replied, "If you have placed yourselves into the hands of Saint Joseph, then you have most certainly placed yourselves in the best of hands."

Angela K., Louisiana

Angela's story starts with a "For Sale" sign in the front yard of her home in Louisiana. Her husband wanted to pursue a job offer in Ohio. She put the family statue of Saint Joseph in the second-story window facing out, and began the Novena to Saint Joseph (see page 87) to sell the house if it be God's will for her family. Not two days into the novena, the neighbors witnessed a ball of lightening hit the window where Saint Joseph's statue stood. The wood around the window splintered as the head of Saint Joseph went sailing through the room. A central wire in the statue grounded the electricity. When a neighbor rang the door bell telling Angela what had just happened, she ran upstairs. Seeing Saint Joseph's head on the rug of the room and the rest of the statue smoking on the windowsill, she promptly went outside and removed the "For Sale" sign. The family didn't move to Ohio.

A friend of theirs also decided to pray this novena to sell the friend's home. It had been on the market for a while. The day someone stood in the yard shaking hands for a deal on the house, their young son came out of the house and said, "This card just fell off the table." It was the same novena card to Saint Joseph.

Sister Maria Elizabeth B., Texas

Sister Elizabeth's memories of growing up are marked in particular by her father's faith in Saint Joseph. She remembers his strong devotion to the foster father of Jesus and provider for the Holy Family. In fact, as he raised his family in San Antonio, Texas, he would often call on Señor San José. "Let's put faith," he would tell his family in challenging times. "God never abandons us. We will do our part, and Señor San José will find a way to provide for us."

In the early 1980s there were six children in the family. Mr. B. worked hard as a contractor on a luxury condominium construction project in the Texas hill country. In parts of Texas, many investors in real estate developments were from Mexico. With the devaluation of the Mexican peso, the industry halted. Mr. B. found himself out of work, and the family lost everything, including their own home. Miraculously, they did not end up on the street. They were able to get an apartment in the city, and neighbors or parishioners would bring them food. There were many days when Sister Elizabeth's parents had no idea how they would feed their children, but still they had trust in Saint Joseph to provide for them. Unfailingly, when they most needed it, someone would ring the doorbell and drop off a large block of cheese or a sack of beans. Two women who worked at one of the hotels in downtown San Antonio would often bring the leftovers from the buffets to the family.

"We had nothing," Sister Elizabeth remembers, "and things would appear just when we needed them. My father was looking for a job, and he would often plead with Saint Joseph to provide for his family. Then he would tell us not to worry. Saint Joseph would provide for us. And through the miraculous goodness of God, we came through those difficult years and were eventually able to buy an older home in a poorer neighborhood. We learned how to value the most essential things in life — especially one another. Even to this day we have a fond devotion to this powerful saint."

ELIZABETH P., VIRGINIA

Elizabeth is the mother of three boys and five girls. The delivery of the last four children she entrusted to Saint Joseph. Elizabeth figured that if he could get Mary to Bethlehem on time for the birth of her baby, Jesus, he was the right saint to take care of getting her to the hospital on time. Before each baby was due, she began a thirty-day novena to Saint Joseph. She and her husband live about an hour from the hospital, and the morning rush-hour traffic can be horrendous. It was Saint Joseph's job to schedule delivery at another time of day and make sure she could get to the hospital safely and on time.

As her daughter Philomena's birth approached, Elizabeth asked Saint Joseph for the baby to be born about a half hour after they got to the hospital. Philomena was born forty-five minutes after they arrived at the hospital. Early morning hours. No traffic.

Ian was born just after midnight following a few hours of labor. No traffic worries there, either.

Faustina was in a posterior position, making her delivery more difficult. She was born about forty-five minutes after her mother got to the hospital. If she hadn't been in that position, she might have been born in the car on the way, because on their trip to the hospital Elizabeth and her husband had been pulled over by the police for speeding. Faustina also was born before rush hour.

Miriam's birth was the most amazing. Rush hour was beginning, and Elizabeth was trying to decide whether she should go to the hospital or wait for traffic to calm. She prayed to Saint Joseph, and she felt that he told her to go. So off went she and her husband, winding their way through the morning commute. After she arrived at the hospital, a couple of hours passed, and Elizabeth was beginning to wonder why Saint Joseph had sent her to the hospital so soon. Then her labor intensified and Miriam came so fast that if Elizabeth had waited until she was absolutely sure it was time, she would never have made it to the hospital. Once again Saint Joseph knew what he was doing!

Jean M., Missouri

On a trip to see the Carmelites in Denver, Jean's family's car broke down on a deserted highway.

There was no other car in sight. Her mother began a novena to Saint Joseph, and soon a young man approached the car, asking if he could help. No one saw where he had come from. "I have a gas station in town," he offered. The town wasn't even visible from the highway. After getting the car to his shop, he just happened to have the exact part their car needed. He replaced the damaged part, and the car was ready to go. Jean's mom and dad turned to thank him, but he was nowhere to be found.

Sister Sharon Anne L., Massachusetts

Sister Sharon and several other sisters visited Mr. Jablonski, the elderly father of one of the sisters in our community. They had gathered to pray the rosary with the immediate family and to keep vigil at his bedside, as he was near death. Mr. Jablonski's breathing was heavy, and he was very agitated. Sister Sharon felt inspired to pray to Saint Joseph and repeated in her heart a prayer to the great saint to grant Mr. Jablonski a happy death. "O Saint Joseph," she prayed, "foster father of Jesus Christ and true spouse of the Virgin Mary, pray for us and for the dying of this day." After a few hours they left. All the way home and during the night she prayed confidently to Saint Joseph. The following

morning, Mr. Jablonski's daughter called the community to say that after the sisters' visit, her father
had relaxed and that he had died serenely during the
night.

Glenn S., Florida

The family's first tears fell at the words of the
doctor that their father's life would soon be over.
Glenn's dad, Harold, had cancer. The prognosis:
two weeks to two months.

For 51 years, Harold had been married to
Maria, mother of his four children and grandmoth-
er of nine. Then 34, Glenn was the youngest son.
Through good times and bad, Maria and Harold
had always put their family before everything else.
Even, actually, *before* each other. Glenn's mom and
dad had made it through a marriage of arguing and
miscommunication, but with this news, Glenn, his
mother, and his siblings were all about to witness
the power of the sacrament of Matrimony.

On the first night home from the hospital
Maria cried on her son Glenn's shoulder, "Your
father's never told me that he loves me," she told
him with immense hurt in her eyes. "All I want is
those words to come out of his mouth, but all he
says is, 'You know I do.' Why can't he tell me?"

Glenn decided to stay with his parents in Biloxi, Mississippi, traveling periodically back to New Orleans, where he ran his own company as a graphic artist. Each day began with Mass, then family members took turns talking and listening to what their father had to tell them. As the days passed, Harold opened his heart to his family, one after another, in every way.

Gradually, Harold's jaundice was accompanied by increasing pain and weakness. The medications could not provide total relief. The family struggled. They wanted their father to be as comfortable as possible, and yet they were afraid of losing him to the numbness and comatose state they had heard would accompany higher doses of morphine. They were not ready to lose their dad before he left them; there was too much still to say and do.

Glenn had to return to New Orleans for three weeks to take care of business. He was afraid that his father would not hang on until he returned. The anxiety was unbearable. "Good Saint Joseph...." he prayed. One day Glenn went to his parish to request a Mass for his father and to light a candle before a statue of Saint Joseph. The secretary gave him a box of old prayer cards to Saint Joseph, and he began giving them to all his friends, asking them to pray for his father's happy and peaceful death.

Glenn burned his own candle at both ends, cramming a three-month project into three weeks so he could get back to his family as soon as possible. He prayed, and his friends prayed. Meanwhile, the family gathered around Harold to share nursing responsibilities. When he eventually had to use a wheelchair, Harold actually loved every minute of it. He never had been one to sit around the house for long, and now he reminded them every so often, "How about let's go take a ride."

Harold's health began to deteriorate badly. His mind was coming and going. His body was shutting down. It was hard for Glenn to watch what was happening to his father. At the same time, however, he was beginning to know his dad's heart for the first time. On one of Harold's last days, Glenn knelt beside his dad's bed and cried as he recited the Chaplet of Divine Mercy. In his heart he prayed again and again the words Jesus had taught Saint Faustina, *My Jesus, I trust in you*. Rising, he leaned over and kissed his dad and told him how much he loved him. Then Glenn impishly told him he was going to play the Hank Williams tape that his dad had made them listen to over and over again on their car trips when they were younger. Glenn's mother, sister, and brother-in-law Tom had come in the room to be with him. They all laughed as Glenn pressed the play button. Harold reacted to the music by squeezing his wife's hand. Needless to say, Hank played all night.

And then came Friday, the solemnity of the Sacred Heart of Jesus. Their dad's struggle was nearing its end. Reactions from him were very few. Prayers were constant, and the family's vigil continued through the night. Glenn's mother and sister slept closest to Harold. At around 2:00 the next morning, Glenn was awakened by his sister with a simple "I need your help with Dad." From then until 6:20 P.M. they worked to make their dad as comfortable as possible. Glenn began to doubt they would see the peaceful and happy death he had been praying for. "What's going on, Saint Joseph?" was all he could think.

The visitors kept coming as the family continued trying to make their dad as comfortable as possible. Then came Harold's hour of death on the feast of the Immaculate Heart of Mary. Glenn's brother-in-law announced that he could feel the angels all around them, so everyone gathered in the room around their father. Holding tight to the right hand of the man God had given her, his mother led them in the Lord's Prayer.

"When you get to heaven, tell my mom and dad hello for me," said Tom, Glenn's brother-in-law, "and that I love them. And make sure you pray for us all, Paw Paw," as he affectionately called the grandfather of his two girls.

"Okay," uttered Harold. "Okay!" they all shouted through their tears and amazement.

"I love you, Harold. I love you, Harold," repeated their mom.

"I love you too," replied their father, from the very depths of his heart. Joy filled the room! Unbelievable joy! They all heard it. They all repeated it. Harold had said, "I love you too!" Somehow he had found the strength to give their mom her last and most beautiful gift.

With Tom continuing to insist about the angels, they all stayed affixed to their dad's bedside. He was beginning to move his body again for the first time in three days as he attempted to sit forward while raising his hands toward the ceiling. They tried to hold him down, not realizing that he was reaching for something they could not see. Their parish priest, Father Quinn, arrived to administer the sacrament of Anointing of the Sick, and Harold sat up and opened his eyes one last time.

Miraculously, after three months of jaundice, they were once again beautifully clear. He reached up, then lay back down and stopped breathing. As

Father Quinn anointed him, Harold took a few more breaths and expired.

The peace was incredible. It felt to Glenn as if his father's spirit passed right through him on his way to heaven, leaving him with an overwhelming sense of peace. Opening his eyes, he gazed at the Eucharist in the priest's hands. "Would you receive your dad's last Communion?" he asked him. "Yes," Glenn said. Glenn received this awesome gift with gratitude to God for his love and mercy that had taken them on an amazing and otherwise impossible journey.

Walking out of the house, Glenn could not help but raise his arms high in the symbol of victory as he saw dad's best fishing buddy, Frank, coming up the walk. He knew Frank would understand. Glenn told him, "I wish I could have seen the sky above the house when Dad died, because it opened up and brought him home."

Through all of the pain and suffering of those last few days, Saint Joseph had brought his own family to Glenn's and had brought them all home by God's power in the Risen Lord.

Prayers to Saint Joseph

Pray to Saint Joseph confidently and faithfully. He can help us, and he wants to do so. His heart is full of love and goodness, and he responds to everyone with fatherly generosity.

— Don G. Pasquali, SSP

FOR FAMILIES AND HOMES

Prayer for One's Family

*H*eavenly Father, I thank you for the gift of my family and for the many joys and blessings that have come to me through each of them. Help me to appreciate the uniqueness of each while celebrating the diversity of all. Through the intercession of Saint Joseph, foster father of your Son, I ask you to protect my family from the evils of this world. Grant us all the power to forgive when we have been hurt and the humility to ask for forgiveness when we have caused pain. Unite us in the love of your Son, Jesus, so that we may be a sign of the unity you desire for all humanity.

Saint Joseph, intercede for us. Amen.

Prayer to Obtain a Special Favor

O glorious Saint Joseph, steadfast follower of Jesus Christ, I am confident that your prayers for me will be graciously heard at the throne of God. To you I lift my heart and hands, asking your powerful intercession to obtain from the compassionate heart of Jesus all the graces necessary for my spiritual and temporal well-being, particularly the grace of a happy death, and the special grace for which I now pray *(mention your request).*

Saint Joseph, guardian of the Word Incarnate, by the love you bear for Jesus Christ, and for the glory of his name, hear my prayer and obtain my petitions. Amen.

Prayer When a Spouse Has Had an Affair

Saint Joseph, what anguish must have filled your heart when you found that Mary was with child, and you thought of ending your betrothal to her, to "put her away" quietly and not disgrace her. And what profound joy you must have experienced when the mystery of the Incarnation was revealed to you. By this sorrow and joy of yours, I ask that you walk with me through this painful time. You know the anguish and anger, the betrayal and humiliation I feel. Teach me how to surrender to the Lord the moments of painful confusion, to listen with my heart when the Spirit speaks to me so that, like you, I may accomplish all that the Lord has planned for me. Amen.

⎯⎯⎯⎯◦◦◦⎯⎯⎯⎯

Prayer to Ask Saint Joseph to Be One's Father

Saint Joseph, I need a dad. You know that I don't have a father. I can't count on a strong, comforting, and wise guide to protect and care for me. I feel alone. Would you be my father? Would you do for me all that you did for Jesus? Would you provide the fathering I never had? Would you prepare me for life, even though I am all grown up? Would you teach me to love Jesus the way you did? Would you provide for me, teaching me how to make my life in this world with dignity, justice, and peace? Would you help me have a meaningful life, a depth of soul, and strength of character that would allow me to completely fulfill my life's mission entrusted to me by God?

I feel now that I am not alone. You are my foster father, given to me by God. Thank you for hearing my prayer. Amen.

Prayer of a Father

Saint Joseph, foster father of Jesus, pray for me. Like you, I am a father, provider, protector, mentor, and spouse. Teach me the virtues of trust, prayer, and confidence in God's plan for me and my family. Show me how to form in my children the virtues you instilled in Jesus. Fill me with respect and love for their mother as you loved and respected Mary. Saint Joseph, pray me and for all fathers. Amen.

Prayer of a Divorced Father

Saint Joseph, the pain I feel is more than I can bear. I know you understand, because you once contemplated divorcing Mary quietly when you realized she was with child and the baby wasn't yours. An angel was sent by God to help you understand what

God wanted of you in that situation. Send me an angel to help me find God's direction in my life right now. I am worried about my kids. I don't know what the future holds. I am embarrassed and don't fit in with my friends anymore. Teach me how to pray. Strengthen me through the Church's ministry. Send me friends who will comfort and understand me. Protect my children and help them to grow up in the security of knowing that I love them and God loves them. Saint Joseph, I too need a father's guidance right now, and I trust in you. Saint Joseph, pray for me. Amen.

<hr />

Prayer of a Father for His Children

Saint Joseph, you were the foster father of Jesus and taught the Son of God everything from virtues to woodworking to how to pray. You protected him from harm, found him when he was lost, and provided for him as he grew up. Teach me how to be a good father. Show me how to practice and teach my children the virtues of faith, hope, and love, courage, obedience, and love for the poor. As they grow up and choose their direction in life, lead me in giving them good advice. Let my children see me praying, and give me the courage and confidence to pray with them. Protect my children from harm as you once protected Jesus from the threats of Herod. Help me keep a job so that I can provide for them and teach them the value of honest work and trust in providence. Saint Joseph, patron of fathers, pray for me. Amen.

Prayer to Sell a House or Property

There are many reasons why people might need to sell their house or property and do so quickly: job transfers, career changes, academic opportunities, increase or decrease in family size, and relocation of an aging parent or a disabled family member.

Dear Saint Joseph, help me to sell this house (or property) quickly. I ask you to intercede for me with the Heavenly Father. I ask for the grace of prudence, that I may make wise decisions regarding this sale, and for the virtue of justice, that I act in a manner worthy of a follower of Christ. Amen.

Prayer to Find a New Home

Dear Saint Joseph, intercede for me with the Heavenly Father, that I might find a new home for my family. I need a place that is sufficient for our needs in an area that is safe for my family. I know you understand the urgency of my request and the anxieties that accompany my search. Rome's census forced you and the Virgin Mary from your home in Nazareth. In Bethlehem, you had difficulty finding lodging for your pregnant wife. To save the Son of God from Herod's wrath, you were forced to leave your homeland and take refuge in a land surrounded by a culture and religion that were foreign to you.

You patiently waited for the death of Herod before you returned to Nazareth with Jesus and Mary. Saint Joseph, help me to be patient in my need, knowing that God will provide in due time. Amen.

Short Petition to Find a New Home

Saint Joseph, hear my prayer. I need to find a new home as quickly as possible. Please intercede for me with the Heavenly Father who knows all our needs. Provider of the Holy Family, pray for us. Amen.

———◦◦◦◦———

Ritual for Those Moving to a New Home: Blessing of Memories

Change in life is inevitable. Anyone moving to a new home, changing schools, or starting a new job knows that it can be a source of anxiety and sadness as well as a source of joyful anticipation.

Reflecting together as a family on the memories made in a home you are moving out of can help tie up the loose threads of your family's lives and lessen the anxiety of departure from a safe space and familiar neighborhood. At a convenient time before the final departure, gather together in your family's favorite room or space (such as a living room, recreation room, or patio).

You will need a Bible, crucifix, or picture of Jesus, Mary, or Joseph. Candles and blessed holy water could be included. Have family members participate in the ritual by holding the various items. Young children could hold their favorite toy.

Leader: In the name of the Father, and of the Son, and of the Holy Spirit.

Family: Amen.

Leader: As we take this last journey, this last walk through our home, let us ask Joseph, Mary, and

Jesus to accompany us as we recall our life here together. They understand the uncertainties of the unknown — first in Bethlehem for the census with no suitable accommodations to be had, then forced to flee to Egypt in order to protect the life of the little Jesus. Several years passed before an angel advised Joseph that it was safe to return home — and Joseph chose obscure Nazareth as a place of safety for his family, where the child Jesus grew in wisdom, age, and grace.

We have lived in this home for *(number)* years and have experienced many moments of peace and happiness, as well as heartaches and difficulties.

For all those times, good and bad, we say:

Family: Thank you, Lord, for the mercy you have shown us.

Leader: Let us now think of those memories that make us glad.

Pause for a few moments and allow the participants to express a remembrance if they so wish. After each memory is expressed, respond with:

Family: Thank you, Lord, for the mercy you have shown us.

When everyone has finished:

Leader: For those moments of joy, let us say:

Leader: Glory to the Father, and to the Son, and to the Holy Spirit …

Family: As it was in the beginning, is now, and ever shall be. Amen.

Holding up the Bible or crucifix, make the sign of the cross. If blessed holy water is available, sprinkle the room and proceed to the next until all rooms have been visited. As the blessing of the room takes place:

Family: Glory to the Father, and to the Son, and to the Holy Spirit, as it was in the beginning, is now, and ever shall be. Amen.

As the family proceeds to the next room, they could say:

Family: As for me and my house, we will serve the Lord.

Or sing a verse of a favorite hymn.
When the pilgrimage through the house is finished:

Leader: Holy Joseph, you are proclaimed patron and protector of the universal Church.

Guard this family that we may always be true witnesses of your Son. Amen.

FOR FINANCIAL NEEDS AND FOR THOSE SEEKING EMPLOYMENT

In Times of Financial Stress

*H*oly Joseph, help me to choose wisely in these difficult times of economic instability. Let my decisions be motivated by true need and justice toward my neighbor. May they always be anchored in charity.

Help me to remember that real security comes from trusting in God's goodness and mercy — "Seek first the kingdom of heaven and all else will be given you besides."

Saint Joseph, provide for me. Amen.

For a Family Person Seeking Employment

*S*aint Joseph, foster father of Jesus and spouse of the Virgin Mary, help me to find suitable work, with adequate pay and health benefits for myself and family. You know the anxiety that I feel as I search for means to support myself and my family.

As head of a household, you understand my needs to be able to provide for my family, to pay my just debts with dignity, and to help others who are also in need. Teach me to trust in God as a loving Father as you did. Saint Joseph, saint of Divine Providence, intercede for me! Amen.

For a Single Person Seeking Employment

Saint Joseph, saint of Divine Providence, help me to find suitable work that provides adequate pay and benefits so that I might be able to pay my just debts with dignity and to help others who are in need. Saint Joseph, teach me to trust in God's loving Providence.

Holy Joseph, saint of Divine Providence, intercede to God for me in all my needs! Amen.

A Worker's Prayer

Saint Joseph, example for all those who work to support themselves and their families, obtain for me the grace to labor with gratitude and joy. Grant that I may consider my daily endeavors as opportunities to use and develop the gifts of nature and grace I have received from God. In the workplace may I mirror your virtues of integrity, moderation, patience, and inner peace, treating my co-workers with kindness and respect. May all I do and say lead others to the Lord and bring honor to God's name. Amen.

───❧❦❧───

Prayer in Time of Need

Saint Joseph, patron of all who serve God in simplicity of heart and steadfast devotion, ask the Lord to fill my heart with the fire of his love. Awaken within me the virtues of integrity, simplicity, reverence, and gentleness, so that I may radiate God's love to those around me. Intercede for me in my time of particular need, and obtain for me the favor I ask *(mention your request)*. Blessed Joseph, be my protector in life and my consoler at the moment of death. Amen.

───❧❦❧───

Prayer in Time of Difficulty

*H*oly Joseph, with steadfast confidence I come before you seeking your compassion and support. With fatherly care you accompanied and protected Jesus during his childhood. With the love and devotion of a spouse you cherished Mary, his Mother. Now, through your intercession, assist me in this time of adversity. By the love you had for Jesus and Mary on earth, I ask you to console me in my distress and present my petition to our heavenly Father *(mention your request)*.

Lord, give me the spirit of Joseph so that even amid my own hardships I can look beyond myself and reach out to others who are alone and suffering, and thus be an instrument of your love and compassion. Amen.

FOR THOSE SUFFERING FROM CATASTROPHES

Prayer in Dark Times

To you, blessed Joseph, we come in our trials, and having asked the help of your most holy spouse, we confidently ask your patronage also. Through that love which bound you to the Immaculate Virgin Mother of God, and through the fatherly care with which you embraced the child Jesus, we humbly beg you to look kindly upon the inheritance which Jesus Christ has purchased by his blood, and to aid us in our necessities with your power and strength *(mention your request)*.

Most watchful guardian of the Holy Family, defend the followers of Jesus Christ; most loving father, defend us against the attacks of the evil one and assist us in our struggle against the power of darkness. As once you rescued the child Jesus from danger, so now protect God's holy Church from the power of Satan and from all harm. Shield, too, each one of us by your constant protection, so that, supported by your example and your help, we may live

as dedicated followers of Jesus Christ, die a holy
death, and obtain eternal happiness in heaven. Amen.

Adapted from common sources

Memorare to Saint Joseph

Remember, O most chaste spouse of the Virgin
Mary, that never has it been known that anyone
who asked for your help or sought your intercession
was left unaided. Inspired by this confidence, I
commend myself to you and beg your protection.
Despise not my petition, dear foster father of our
Redeemer, but hear and answer my prayer. Amen.

From common sources

Prayer When Threatened
by Natural Disasters

Saint Joseph, while chosen by God to be the foster
father of the Word made flesh, you still suffered distress at having to accept a stable's shelter for Mary to

give birth and then flee to Egypt, where you stayed for many years far from your home. But the deprivation you experienced must have turned to joy when you heard angels heralding the birth of the Savior.

By this sorrow and joy of yours, I ask you to intercede before the Lord for those who suffer the destruction of their homes and property; who have had to evacuate from oncoming storms, fires, or earthquakes; and who are without food and shelter for themselves and their families.

Comfort those in evacuation shelters, calm the fears of those who worry about their relatives in harm's way, give prudence and strength to civil leaders and emergency personnel, and protect the children. As you generously sought to make Mary and Jesus safe and comfortable, encourage those who have not been affected or displaced to provide for those who are suffering so they do not feel themselves alone as they pick up the pieces of their lives. Give them the grace to discover the miraculous ways in which Jesus is with them, even at this time. Saint Joseph, provide for them. Amen.

FOR SPIRITUAL NEEDS
AND FOR THE CHURCH

Prayer to Grow in Devotion to Mary

Saint Joseph, pure spouse of Mary, we humbly ask you to obtain for us a true devotion to our tender Mother, Teacher, and Queen. By divine will, your mission was associated to Mary's. With Mary you shared sufferings and joys; with her there was a holy rivalry in virtue, work, and merits; with her you were united in mind and heart. Saint Joseph, obtain for us the grace to know the Blessed Virgin Mary, to imitate her, to love her, to pray to her always. Draw many souls to her maternal heart. Amen.

Blessed James Alberione

Saint Joseph, Patron of the Church

Saint Joseph, be our protector. May your interior spirit of peace, silence, good work, and prayer for the cause of Holy Church always be our inspiration. May your spirit bring us joy in union with your blessed spouse, our sweet and gentle Immaculate Mother, and in the strong yet tender love of Jesus, the glorious and immortal King of all ages and peoples. Amen.

Blessed Pope John XXIII

------------⟨᳔⟩------------

Prayer for Spiritual Growth

Saint Joseph, we bless the Lord for choosing you to be the one to raise the Son of God. You loved Jesus with a father's love, and he loved you with the love of a son. You held him in your arms and helped him take his first steps. You heard his first words and taught him his prayers. By faith you adored in him the Incarnate Son of God, while he obeyed you, served you, listened to you. You held pleasant conversations with him and shared work, great sufferings, and most tender consolations.

Obtain for us the grace never to offend Jesus by sin. Pray for us that we may nourish ourselves often at the Eucharist and experience Jesus' mercy in the sacrament of Reconciliation. Through your prayers may we attain to a great intimacy with Jesus and a tender and strong love for him while on earth, so that we might possess him forever in heaven. Amen.

Adapted from Blessed James Alberione

Prayer of Praise and Thanksgiving

Lord Jesus, I praise, glorify, and bless you for all the graces and privileges you have bestowed upon Joseph, your foster father and servant. By his merits grant me your grace, and through his intercession help me in all my needs. At the hour of my death be with me until that time when I can join the saints in heaven to praise you forever and ever. Amen.

Te Ioseph

*(Traditional Latin hymn to Saint Joseph
followed by an English translation.)*

Te, Ioseph, celebrent agmina caelitum;
Te cuncti resonent Christiadum chori:
Qui clarus meritis junctus et inclytae
Casto foedere Virgini.

Almo cum tumidam germine coniugem
Admirans, dubio tangeris anxius,
Afflatu superis Flaminis Angelus
Conceptum puerum docet.

Tu natum Dominum stringis, ad exteras,
Aegypti profugum tu sequeris plagas;
Amissum Solymis, qaeris et invenis;
Miscens gaudia fletibus.

Post mortem reliquos sors pia consecrat,
Palmamque emeritos gloria suscipit:
Tu vivens, Superis par, frùeris Deo,
Mira sorte beatior.

Nobis, summa Trias, parce precantibus,
Da Ioseph meritis sidera scandere:
Ut tandem liceat nos tibi perpetim,
Gratum promere canticum. Amen.

O Joseph, to you sing angel choirs joyously;
In merits you abound,
Christians give you great praise.
United to your spouse, Virgin Immaculate,
By that bond holy and most chaste.

You felt amazement and deepest anxiety,
Seeing your spouse with child,
till the doubt was relieved.
An angel reassured, told you to have no fear:
"By the Spirit he is conceived."

The newborn King of kings you embraced
        with great joy,
To Egypt followed him, for his sake an exile.
You lost and sought and found him in Jerusalem,
Joys and tears mingled all the while.

Others attain to bliss only after their death;
Glory awaits those who palms of martyrs
        have won.
More blest by far than they: you, living here below,
Enjoyed the presence of God's Son.

Pardon us suppliants, Most Holy Trinity,
May Joseph's merits lead us to beatitude.
Thus and forevermore, we shall sing joyously
Hymns of eternal gratitude.

Litany of Saint Joseph

Lord, have mercy on us.
Christ, have mercy on us.
Lord, have mercy.

Christ, hear us.
   Christ graciously hear us.
God, the Father of heaven,
   have mercy on us.
God, the Son, Redeemer of the world,
   have mercy on us.
God, the Holy Spirit,
   have mercy on us.
Holy Trinity, One God,
   have mercy on us.

Holy Mary,	*pray for us.*
Saint Joseph,	*pray for us.*
Renowned offspring of David,	*pray for us.*
Light of Patriarchs,	*pray for us.*
Spouse of the Mother of God,	*pray for us.*
Chaste guardian of the Virgin,	*pray for us.*
Foster-father of the Son of God,	*pray for us.*
Diligent protector of Christ,	*pray for us.*
Head of the Holy Family,	*pray for us.*
Joseph most just,	*pray for us.*
Joseph most chaste,	*pray for us.*

Joseph most prudent,	*pray for us.*
Joseph most strong,	*pray for us.*
Joseph most obedient,	*pray for us.*
Joseph most faithful,	*pray for us.*
Mirror of patience,	*pray for us.*
Lover of poverty,	*pray for us.*
Model of artisans,	*pray for us.*
Glory of home life,	*pray for us.*
Guardian of virgins,	*pray for us.*
Pillar of families,	*pray for us.*
Solace of the wretched,	*pray for us.*
Hope of the sick,	*pray for us.*
Patron of the dying,	*pray for us.*
Terror of demons,	*pray for us.*
Protector of Holy Church,	*pray for us.*

Lamb of God, who takes away the sins of the world,
   spare us, O Lord!
Lamb of God, who takes away the sins of the world,
   graciously hear us, O Lord!
Lamb of God, who takes away the sins of the world,
   have mercy on us.

V. He made him the lord of his household,

R. And ruler of all his possessions.

   Let us pray:
   O God, in your unspeakable providence, you were pleased to choose Blessed Joseph to be the

spouse of your most holy Mother, grant, we beseech you, that we may deserve to have him as our intercessor in heaven, whom we venerate as our protector on earth; you who live and reign forever and ever. Amen.

⁕

Novena to Saint Joseph

This powerful novena consists of turning to Joseph four times a day and honoring him in four points. It does not matter where or when. Only one point is taken at a time. This novena, going back to Father Louis Lallemant, S.J. (1588–1635), has proven to be highly efficacious.

1. *Saint Joseph's faithfulness to God's grace.* Think of the times in Joseph's life when he responded generously to God's call and inspirations. Thank God, and ask Saint Joseph's help in responding faithfully to God's invitations and grace.

2. *Saint Joseph's fidelity to prayer, listening to God, and virtue.* Reflect on what Joseph must have been like, the way he carried out his daily labor, how he led his family in prayer, what kind of virtue must have marked his daily living. Thank God and ask through Saint Joseph to be faithful to virtue, prayer, and the Christian life.

3. *Saint Joseph's love for Mary.* Imagine the house of Nazareth where Joseph lived with Jesus and Mary. Let his care for her impress itself on your heart. See how he prayed with her, provided for her, and shared with her the responsibility of raising Jesus. Thank God and ask through Saint Joseph the grace to love Mary and to remain close to her all through your life.

4. *Saint Joseph's love for Jesus.* Imagine how much Joseph must have loved Jesus. What was in his heart when Jesus was born, when he took his first steps, said his first words, went to the Temple for the first time, finished building his first table… Thank God and ask through Saint Joseph the grace to love Jesus as he did.

*Adapted from a leaflet published by
the Old Palace, Mayfield, Sussex, England*

Rosary in Honor of Saint Joseph

This set of mysteries of the Rosary contemplates Saint Joseph in relationship with Jesus and Mary.

First Mystery
The Annunciation to Joseph
(Mt 1:18–25)

Just as the Word was announced to you in such power that it changed your life forever, so may the Word penetrate us, changing us and all those who hear us announce it — and announce him.

"My word … shall not return to me empty, / but it shall accomplish that which I purpose, and succeed in the thing for which I sent it" (Is 55:11).

Second Mystery
The Circumcision and Naming of Joseph's Son
(Mt 1:25; Lk 2:21)

Joseph, because of you, we are now on a first name basis with God! *"… through him both of us have access in one Spirit to the Father"* (Eph. 2:18).

Did you understand the significance of what you did? Did you realize who it was that you lifted in your arms? Did you realize, "faithful cooperator in our redemption," that you were preparing "the

Victim, the Priest, the Divine Master of the world?"
(Blessed James Alberione, SSP)

In the way we reach out to others may we do
the same, faithfully continuing what you faithfully
began.

Third Mystery

The Flight into Egypt and the Return
(Mt 2:13–15; 19–23)

You know the pain of uncertainty, unfulfilled
dreams, hopes for love, disappointment, plans gone
awry, and, especially, rejection of the Word. During
these times in our lives, give us courage and creativ-
ity to begin again. Sustain us with deeper love for
Jesus and Mary.

Fourth Mystery

The Losing of Jesus and
Finding Him in the Temple
(Lk 2:41–50)

What must it have been like to lose the Son of
God? What must it have been like to find him
again? You were "astonished." Why? Because he
turned your expectations upside down.

Give us hearts that always seek the Lord and,
when we find him, hearts that ponder his words.

Never let us lose him through sin! Console us when, in our unrealistic expectations, he must disappear. Fill us with wonder and gratitude when we find him where we least expect.

FIFTH MYSTERY

The Hidden Life and the Death of Joseph
(Heb 13:7)

"Open to me the gates of righteousness, that I may enter though them and give thanks to the LORD" (Ps 118:19).

We bless the Lord for the hidden life you shared with Jesus and Mary. As your life drew to a close, what was it like to stand on the threshold of redemption? The trust that had marked your life must now have marked your death.

Give us a holy life and a holy death, full of trust in God's loving care. Save us from a sudden death that catches us unprepared. Come for us, with the two you most cherished in your life.

"Master, now you are dismissing your servant in peace, according to your word; for my eyes have seen your salvation, which you have prepared in the presence of all peoples, a light for revelation to the Gentiles and for glory to your people Israel" (Lk 2:29–32).

A Triduo to Saint Joseph

By John Henry Newman (1801-1890)

FIRST DAY

Consider the glorious titles of Saint Joseph

He was the true and worthy spouse of Mary, supplying in a visible manner the place of Mary's invisible Spouse, the Holy Spirit. He was a virgin, and his virginity was the faithful mirror of the virginity of Mary. He was the cherub, placed to guard the new terrestrial paradise from the intrusion of every foe.

V. Blessed be the name of Joseph.

R. *Henceforth and forever. Amen.*

Let us pray:

God, who in your ineffable Providence did vouchsafe to choose Blessed Joseph to be the husband of your most holy Mother, grant, we beseech you that we may be made worthy to receive him for our intercessor in heaven, whom on earth we venerate as our holy protector; you who live and reign world without end. Amen.

SECOND DAY

Consider the glorious titles of Saint Joseph

His was the title of father of the Son of God, because he was the spouse of Mary, ever Virgin. He was our Lord's father, because Jesus ever yielded to him the obedience of a son. He was our Lord's father, because to him were entrusted, and by him were faithfully fulfilled, the duties of a father in protecting him, giving him a home, sustaining and rearing him, and providing him with a trade.

V. Blessed be the name of Joseph.

R. *Henceforth and forever. Amen.*

Let us pray:

God, who in your ineffable Providence did vouchsafe to choose Blessed Joseph to be the husband of your most holy Mother, grant, we beseech you that we may be made worthy to receive him for our intercessor in heaven, whom on earth we venerate as our holy protector; you who live and reign world without end. Amen.

Third Day

Consider the glorious titles of Saint Joseph

He is Holy Joseph because, according to the opinion of a great number of doctors, he, as well as Saint John Baptist, was sanctified even before he was born. He is Holy Joseph because his office, of being spouse and protector of Mary, specially demanded sanctity. He is Holy Joseph because no other saint but he lived in such and so long intimacy and familiarity with the source of all holiness, Jesus, God incarnate, and Mary, the holiest of creatures.

V. Blessed be the name of Joseph.

R. *Henceforth and forever. Amen.*

Let us pray:

God, who in your ineffable Providence did vouchsafe to choose Blessed Joseph to be the husband of your most holy Mother, grant, we beseech you that we may be made worthy to receive him for our intercessor in heaven, whom on earth we venerate as our holy protector; you who live and reign world without end. Amen.

FOR A HAPPY DEATH

Prayer for a Happy Death

Saint Joseph, protector of the dying, I ask you to intercede for all the dying, and I invoke your assistance in the hour of my own death. You merited a happy passing by a holy life, and in your last hours you had the great consolation of being assisted by Jesus and Mary. Deliver me from sudden death; obtain for me the grace to imitate you in life, to detach my heart from everything worldly, and to gather daily treasures for the moment of my death. Obtain for me the grace to receive well the sacrament of Anointing of the Sick, and with Mary, fill my heart with sentiments of faith, hope, love, and sorrow for sins, so that I may breathe forth my soul in peace. Amen.

Blessed James Alberione

Prayer for the Dying

Saint Joseph, foster father of Jesus Christ and true spouse of the Virgin Mary, pray for us and for those who will die this day (or night).

Afterword:
Becoming Like Joseph

Saint Joseph ...
did you plan how things should be
for the birth of Jesus —
yet, how things unraveled from the first ...
>   an inconvenient census (you wouldn't be at
>   home for the birth),
>   no room in the inn (you failed as a provider
>   for your family),
>   flight into Egypt (you hadn't thought ahead
>   and prepared for this eventuality).

You left town, trade, and tools behind.
Friends and family. Country.
God stripped you of control.
You learned to trust in a generous Father
and to be a generous father.
You, the saint of Divine Providence,

discovered that the provident God
is trustworthy and reliable.

"The birds of the air...
The flowers of the field...
My Father cares for all these ...
He will certainly care for you ...
Do not worry about tomorrow..."

Did Jesus learn all this from you?
Can I?

Additional Resources

Read More About Saint Joseph

Burton, Katherine. *Brother André of Mount Royal.* Notre Dame, Indiana: Ave Maria Press, 1952.

de la Potterie, Ignace, SJ. *Mary in the Mystery of the Covenant.* New York: Alba House, 1992.

Doze, Andrew. *Joseph, Shadow of the Father.* New York: Alba House, 1999.

LaFreniere, Bernard, CSC. *Brother André According to Witnesses.* Montreal: Saint Joseph Oratory, 1990.

BOOKS & MEDIA

A mission of the Daughters of St. Paul

As apostles of Jesus Christ,
evangelizing today's world:

We are CALLED to holiness
by God's living Word and Eucharist.

We COMMUNICATE the Gospel message
through our lives and through all
available forms of media.

We SERVE the Church
by responding to the hopes and needs
of all people with the Word of God,
in the spirit of St. Paul.

For more information visit our website:
www.pauline.org.

Pauline
BOOKS & MEDIA

The Daughters of St. Paul operate book and media centers at the following addresses. Visit, call or write the one nearest you today, or find us on the World Wide Web, www.pauline.org.

CALIFORNIA
3908 Sepulveda Blvd, Culver City, CA 90230 — 310-397-8676
935 Brewster Avenue, Redwood City, CA 94063 — 650-369-4230
5945 Balboa Avenue, San Diego, CA 92111 — 858-565-9181

FLORIDA
145 S.W. 107th Avenue, Miami, FL 33174 — 305-559-6715

HAWAII
1143 Bishop Street, Honolulu, HI 96813 — 808-521-2731
Neighbor Islands call: — 866-521-2731

ILLINOIS
172 North Michigan Avenue, Chicago, IL 60601 — 312-346-4228

LOUISIANA
4403 Veterans Memorial Blvd, Metairie, LA 70006 — 504-887-7631

MASSACHUSETTS
885 Providence Hwy, Dedham, MA 02026 — 781-326-5385

MISSOURI
9804 Watson Road, St. Louis, MO 63126 — 314-965-3512

NEW YORK
64 W. 38th Street, New York, NY 10018 — 212-754-1110

PENNSYLVANIA
Philadelphia—relocating — 215-676-9494

SOUTH CAROLINA
243 King Street, Charleston, SC 29401 — 843-577-0175

VIRGINIA
1025 King Street, Alexandria, VA 22314 — 703-549-3806

CANADA
3022 Dufferin Street, Toronto, ON M6B 3T5 — 416-781-9131

¡También somos su fuente para libros,
videos y música en español!